I wa
a red

by Wendy Body

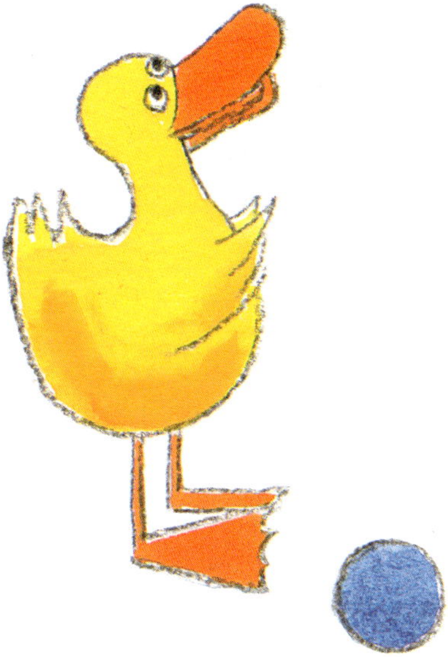
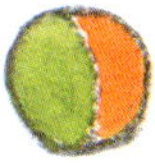

Illustrated by Adrienne Geoghegan

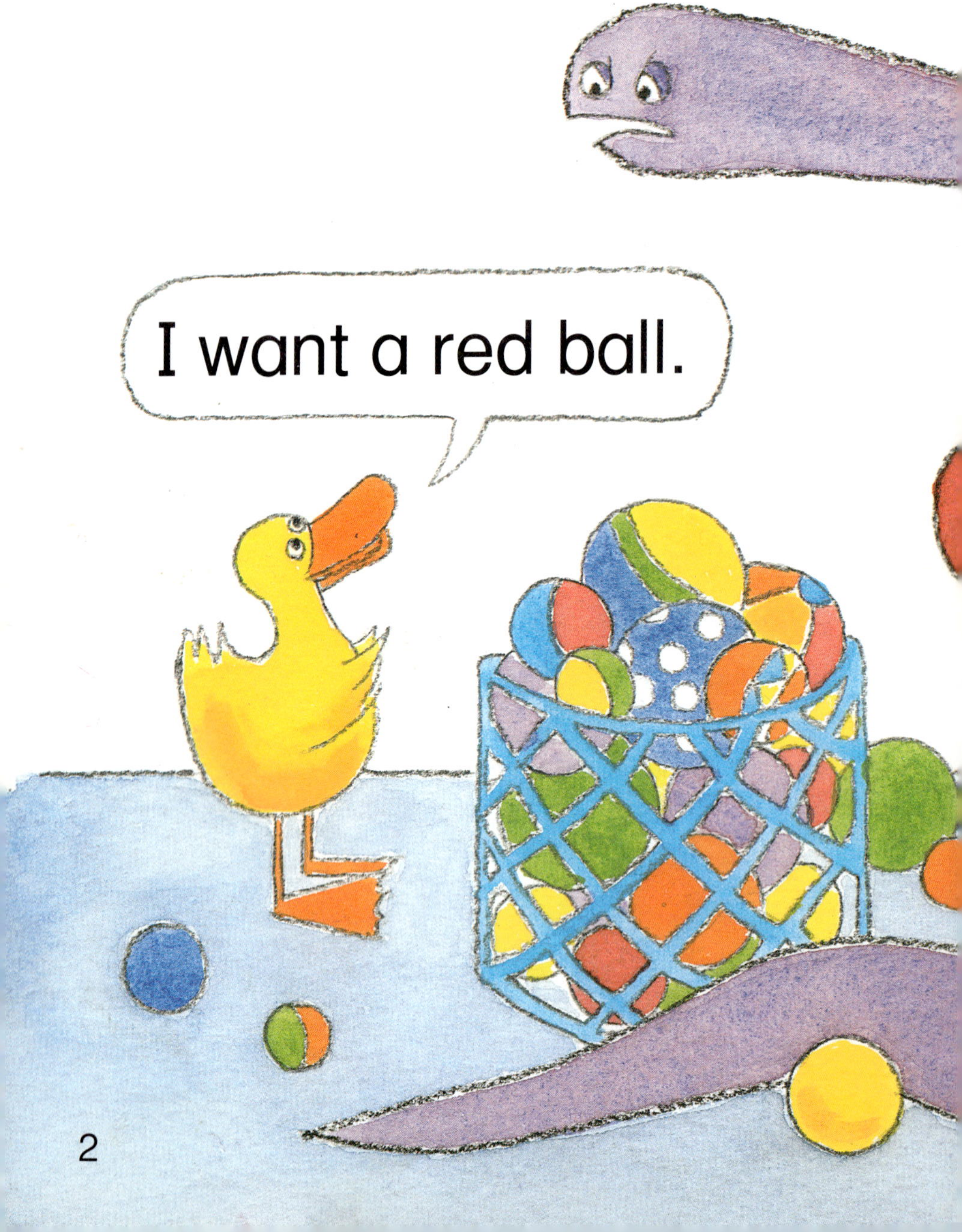
I want a red ball.

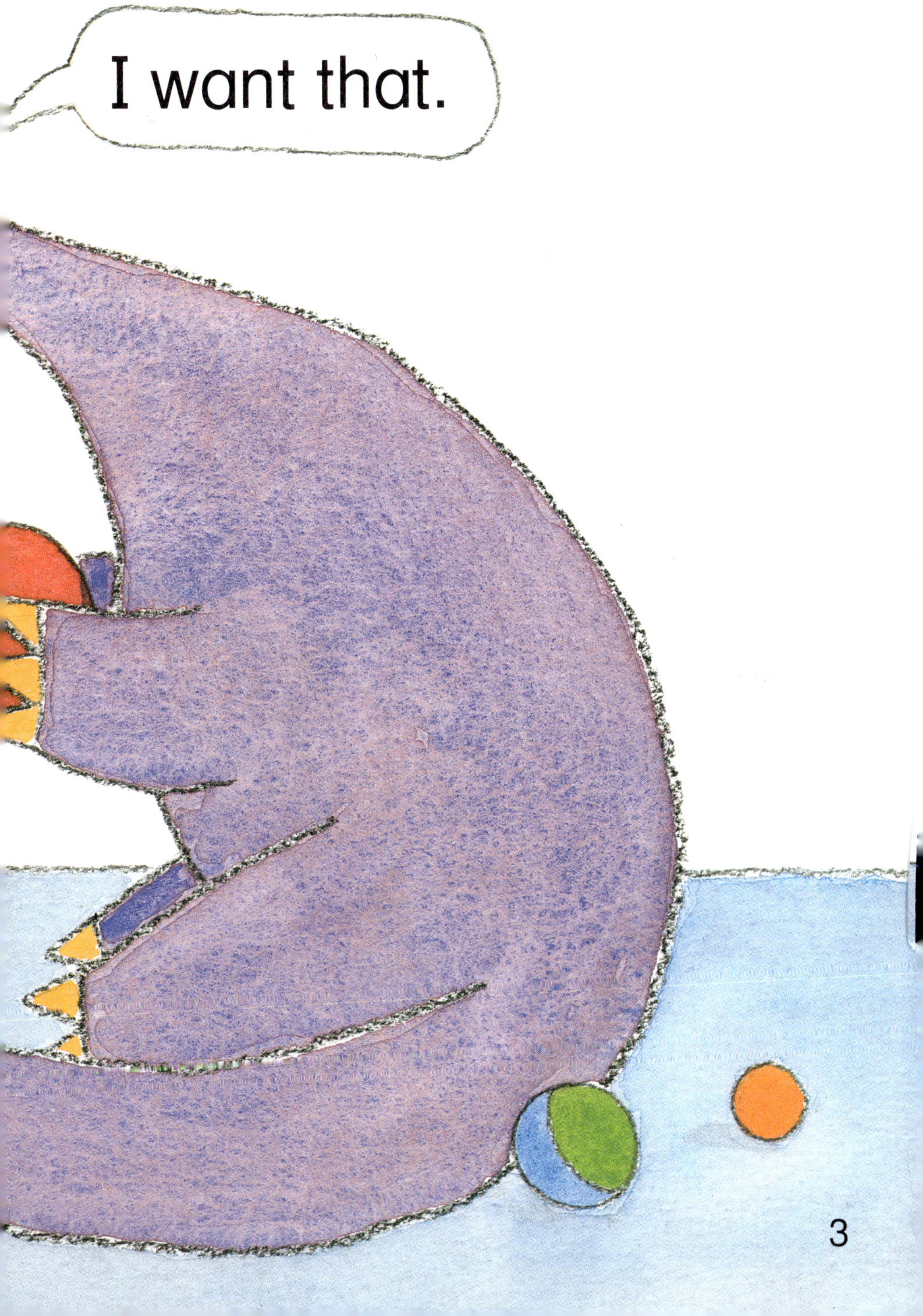
I want that.

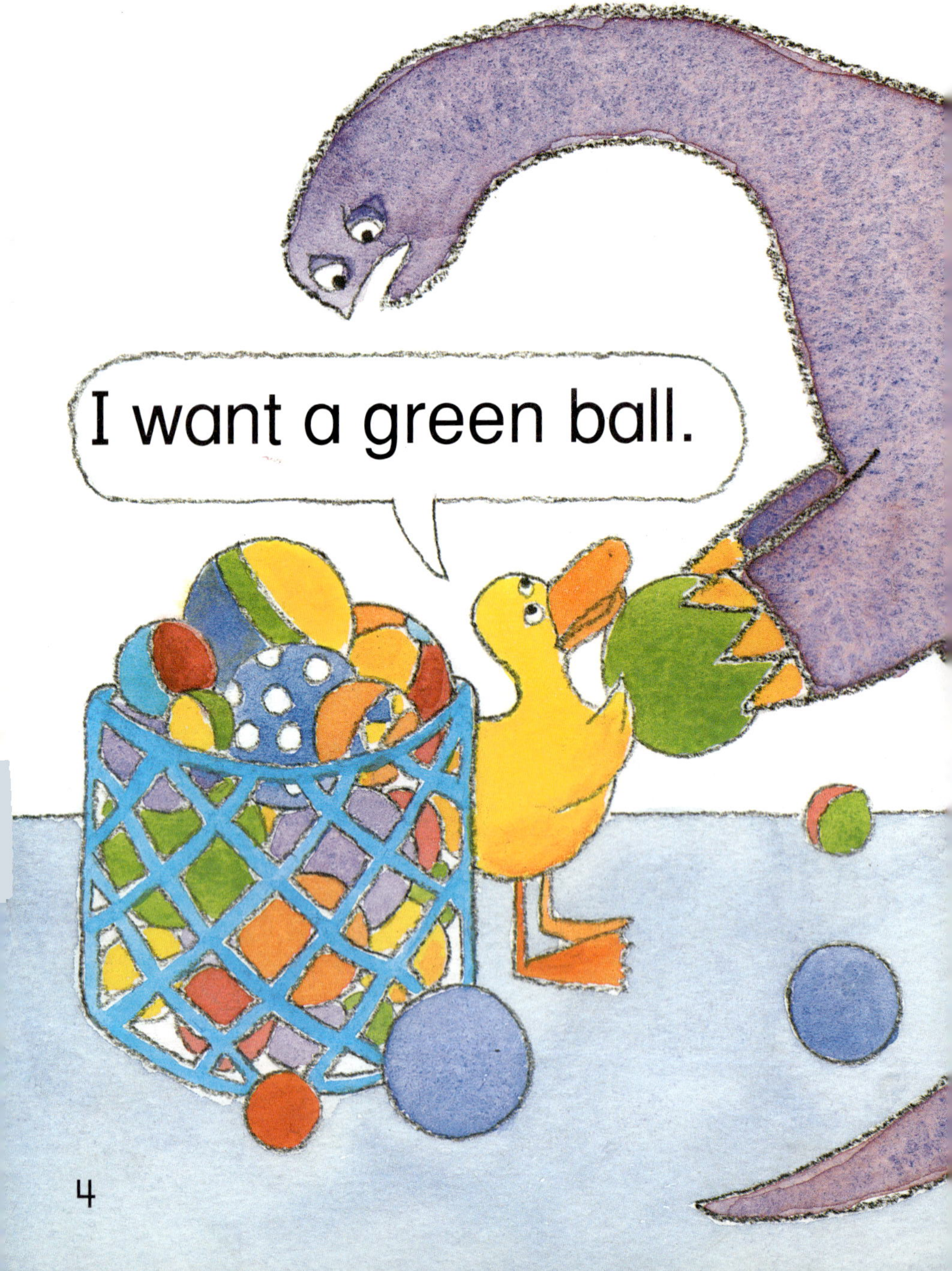
I want a green ball.

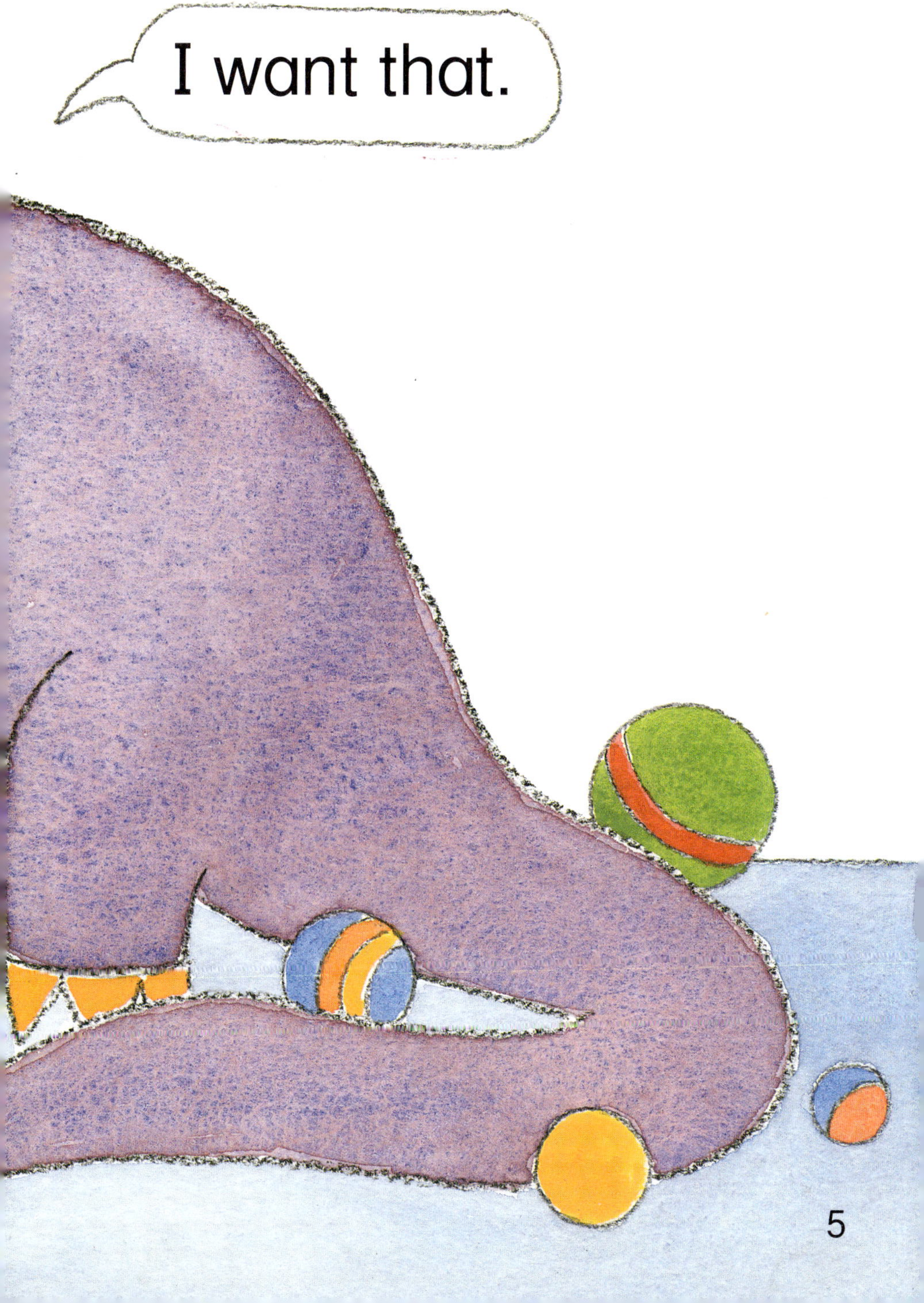
I want that.

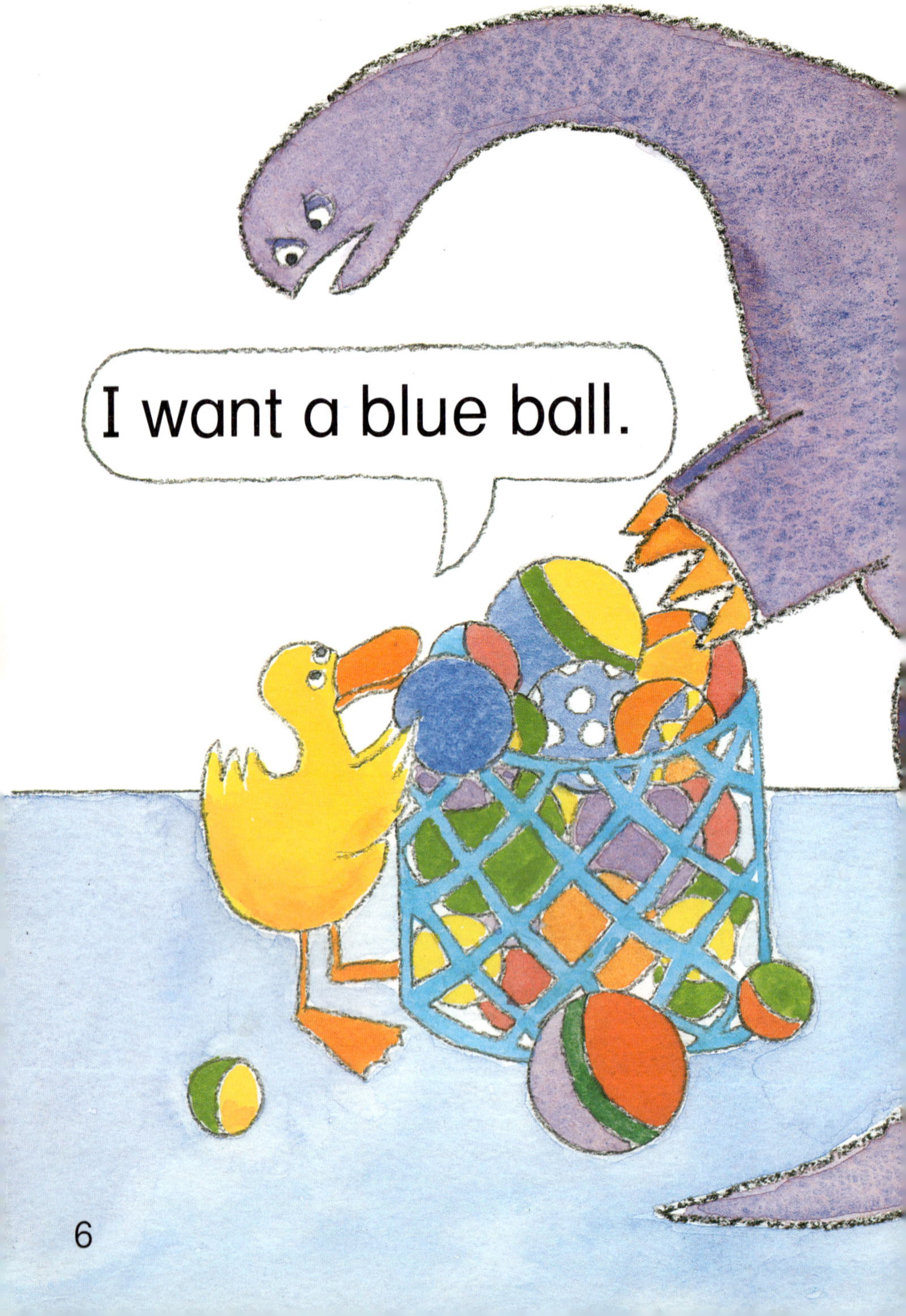
I want a blue ball.

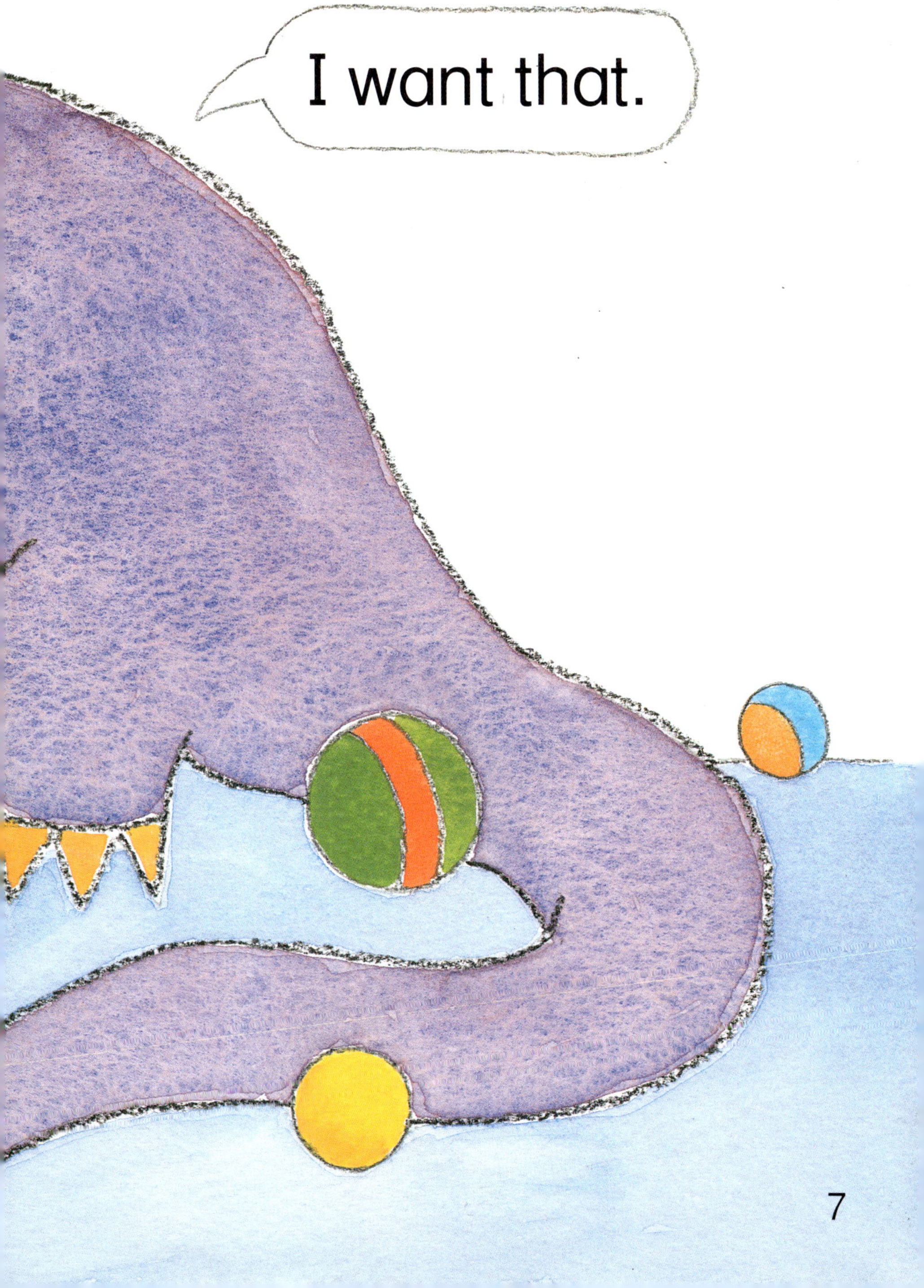
I want that.

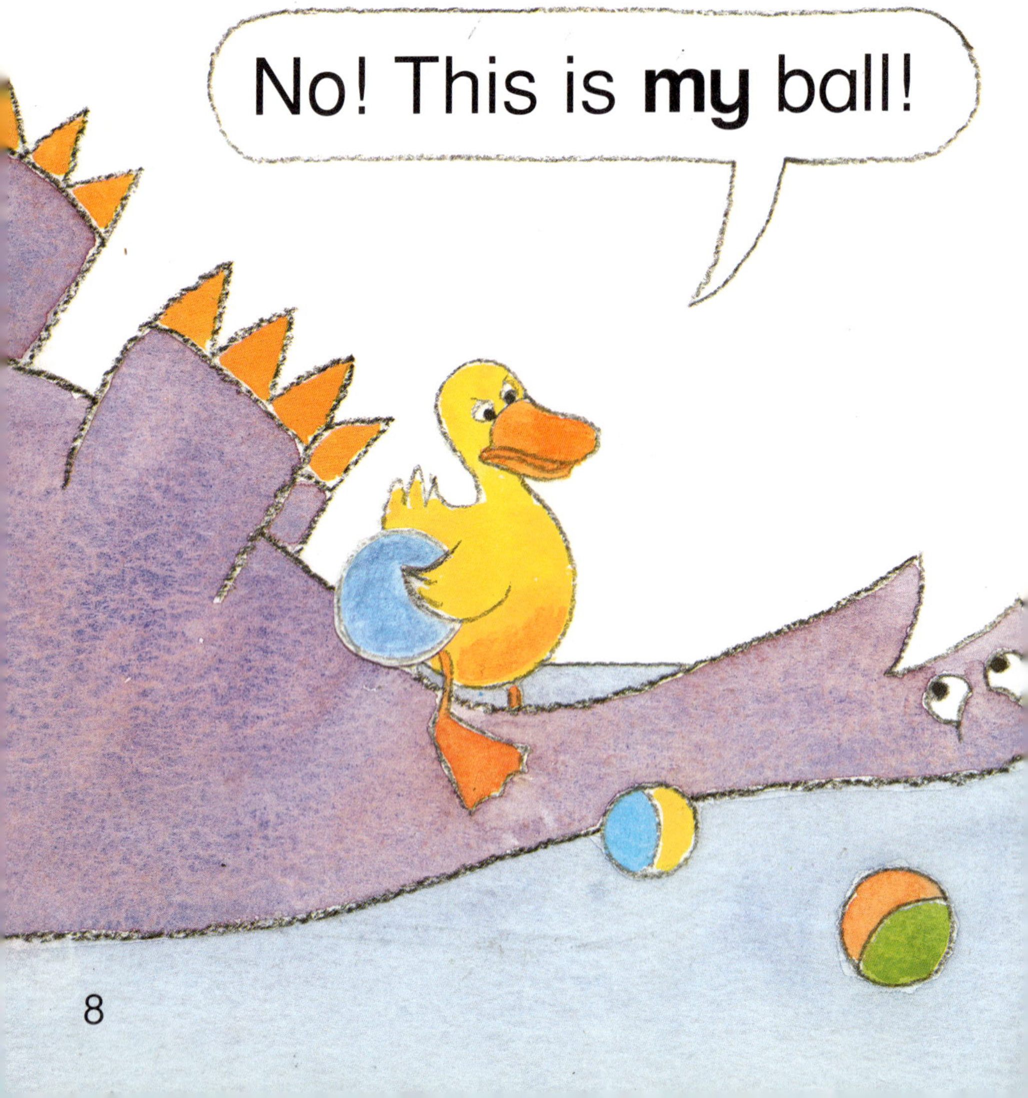
No! This is **my** ball!